Your Idea + My Process puts you in Business.

About the Author: I'm the oldest of 5 siblings 4 boys and 1 girl and she's the baby so you can imagine that she was spoiled rotten. It was sort of my responsibility to be a trail blazer or in my opinion a leader in order to be a good example. So, after high school I joined the USMC now I had no plans to make it a career I wanted to get the GI benefits to go to college. After 3 successful years, I received an honorable discharge moved back to Oklahoma City where I was raised and began my college career.

I knew early in life what I wanted to do which was to become a psychiatrist. I have always been interested in what makes people tick or why they think and do the things they do. So, after graduating from a Jr college by the name of Oscar Rose with a degree in science I transferred to a University named Central State University and as you guessed with a major in psychology and a minor in business.

Well after about 8 months I got caught up in what I call the fast life and my grades began to fade which forced me to change my major to business but even with that after another 6 months I chose to take a break from college and live life a little. Now I didn't tell you that when I got back to OKC my first job was with an Air Force base called Tinker AFB. And I was working and going to school at the same time so I had money and that was one of my distractions.

After 3 years working at Tinker I decided to move to Dallas and I wanted to transfer to another AFB named Carswell but they never had any openings so I chose to resign my position and move to Texas. So I sold everything I owned except my clothes and my car and to Dallas I went. Now some 31 years later I still live there or at least in the suburbs.

I never did become that psychiatrist but I still love to dabble with reading and studying about human nature and other mind developing issues. Today I'm a published author of several books both eBook and paperback formats along with CD's, video's, an online store, I'm a motivational speaker, I have my own podcast show, and just like when I went to college I work full time for the government. And after I retire I will transition into my business full time.

All Rights Reserved. No part of this publication may be reproduced in any form or by any means, including scanning, photo copying, or otherwise without prior written permission of the copyright holder.

Acknowledgements: First I want to thank my God for allowing me the life he has giving me the opportunity to experience many things both good and not so good and still remain standing.

Second, I would like to thank my mother Robbie Morgan for giving me life and nurturing my life in a way that made me the strong and productive man that I am today.

Third, I thank my siblings Michael, Ricky, Ronald, and Donna for forcing me to remain consistent so that they can always look up to me not necessarily to do as I do or as I say but for me to be conscious that someone was always watching.

Forth, I thank my close circle of friends that I've been able to keep for some time now and they know who they are. Now I'm a firm believer that in life we don't get a lot of close friends and because of that I hold mine dear to my heart.

Fifth and finally, I thank my children Jeffery and LaNeetra they have made me extremely happy with the lives they've chosen to create for themselves. Both are college graduated, married with children and they've both given me combined 6 grandchildren. 3 boys and 3 girls, and I feel fantastic that my name will live on and I'm thankful for that.

Alright, now that we've got the formalities out of the way it's time to have some fun. The reason I've decide to write this book is 3-fold.

First as an online business owner you'll want to constantly think in terms of creating products so for me this is another one to add to my list.

Second what I'm going to be teaching you here is exactly the way I set my system up along with some of the mental, physical, and emotional roadblocks you may incur.

Third and finally I'm a speaker and for me it gives me another product to market and sell in the back of the room.

Ok, with that said I want to personally congratulate you for investing in yourself for doing that you have positioned yourself among some of the most successful people on the planet. That's right everyone who's successful are learners they spend money every month, every year, and forever gaining new knowledge to increase their edge.

It's a trait you'll want to consciously work on incorporating into your own system. Fortunately we're in an age where it's never been easier to start your own business and the type of business I help people start are online businesses.

We all know that since we now have Mr. Google we can find information on almost anything we can type into the query box and with Mr. YouTube we can watch a video about anything from A to Z.

Remember, we are in the Information Age and what people want and will pay for is Information, information that you know and are willing to share with them. But not the information you know today. The information you'll learn as you set up the foundation of your online business.

It's true not what you know now but what you'll know in 90 days. Is that a long time to you? Well just imagine how long it took a doctor to become an expert in their field or how long it took a lawyer to become an expert in their field now will you make the money they make after 90 days probably not but keep in mind that you're only in the beginning stages you're only setting up the foundation of your business. Which is what my company teaches you how to do.

Let me ask you a question on a scale from 1 to 10 ten being the most just how important would you say setting up the foundation of your new business is?

Your answer ___

I want to share something very important with you right here if your foundation isn't solid it can't sustain very much growth all in fact if your business suddenly took off and begin to take in large amounts of money you wouldn't have the knowledge of where to put the increase back into your business or what to study next because all that is a process. Which is why I titled this book Your Idea + My Process put you in Business.

Now some of the things I'll cover in this book you won't be able to understand right off and that's mainly because of your knowledge level about the field you'll choose to create a business around. But that's ok that's part of the process it's why if it were easy everyone would be doing it and more so it's why when you do it you're able to live a different life and lifestyle.

I told you that as a young man I knew I wanted to be a psychiatrist well loving the way the mind works has allowed me to study several people, books, videos, audios, and a host of other ways to increase my knowledge about certain things. Increasing my knowledge has led me to understand that it's through sharing that were able to receive what we get on different levels.

You heard it said it's better to give than receive, right? Well it goes to another level once you're able to give to more people and as strange as it may seem once you become comfortable with having the mindset of a giver other opportunities for you will begin to show up in your life.

This journey you're embarking on today is one that will change not only the way you feel about starting a business but also the way you feel about being a better person. I truly believe that the best way to live the life we were created to live requires us to identify for ourselves what our purpose is and to share that purpose with the world.

I also believe that our creator installed within each of us a passion one that only you really know. Although you may be good at a variety of things your passion will stand out for you it will feel easier or more comfortable for you even though it may not be what you're best at you will enjoy it a lot but again only you will really know it.

Table of Contents:

Chapter One: Your Objectives…

Chapter Two: Tools of the Trade…

Chapter Three: Identifying Your Passion…

Chapter Four: Setting up your work area…

Chapter Five: Creating your Products

Chapter Six: Three Things to work on daily…

Chapter Seven: Social Media connections…

Chapter Eight: Marketing and Branding…

Chapter Nine: Your Friends and Family...

Chapter Ten: It's who you become, that matters…

Chapter One: Your Objectives

"Dreams become reality once the dreamer goes beyond imagining and acts them out."

— *Richelle E. Goodrich*

When I speak about your objectives I want you to look at them from a (can do) perspective. What do I mean by that well I mean keep in mind that everything I teach and share with you has been done by other people just like yourself? None of this is rocket science and the process here is only that you understand what to do, do it, then continue to do it.

The online business world is basically repetition once you set everything up. Then you'll figure out what works best for your particular products or services through trial and error. Much of the success involved with your business will be based on timing, timing along with identifying the specific market you want to target.

That will be a few of the areas you'll be able to input your own brand or style into. To distance yourself from the pack. You'll also want to study others who are doing what it is you want to do.

You've probably heard it said that (success leaves clues) right, well that's absolutely true. But if you study only one person you're simply copying his or her style or technique that's not good.

You want to learn from several different sources and several different people. Then create your own style.

Also, the mindset I want you to put yourself in is that of a creator think about the fact that you're not only creating a new business you're also re-creating a new you. Understand this, the more knowledge you have about a certain something the more value you possess and the more value you have the more money you can generate.

But don't get caught up in the money because money is only part of the beauty of owning your own business. What I want you to focus on is the fact that you're doing what you like or maybe even what you love and it's allowing to live the life and lifestyle that you want.

As you become more familiar with the process you'll actually be able to see a change in the way you value your time, or the people you allow in your circle. I share with people all the time that you make a living from 9 to 5 but you create the life you want from 5 to 9.

Think about that for a moment when you get off work on a normal work day how much time between 5 and 9 do you spend learning something? Gaining knowledge about anything most people's answer to that question is zero none.

Let me take that one step further if you were to spend only 30 minutes a day 3 days per week consistently studying something that you already have an interest in just imagine the increase in your knowledge about that something in a short 90 days.

You would have automatically increased your value when it comes to that something you could market yourself as an expert in that niche. Imagine that you an expert. Now the next step after gaining the knowledge is creating products about that niche or area of expertise that you now have and you will create products in the form of information products.

Now I don't want go to deep into products right here because I've dedicated an entire chapter to that later in the book just be ready for a treat when you get to that point.

Now back to objectives as an online business owner you will incorporate a way to build a list. Now in this book I'm teaching from the perspective that you're totally new to the internet, you're totally new to computers, and you're totally new to starting a business so if some of this seems redundant or amateurish just bear with me for a few minutes because remember you to at one time were a beginner. Ok…

With that being said my short answer is your list is your bank. Follow me down this path very quickly if you will. If we both we growing our list and we started at the same time one year ago, and today I have 5000 people on my list and you have 10,000 people on your list which one of us would generate the most money from presenting our products to each list?

Well that's kind of a trick question because initially you probably said you would generate the largest amount of money.

But in reality that may not be the case at all because you may not be taking into consideration the fact that my list is built on my area of expertise and yours on your area of expertise.

For instance, if my area of expertise is photography and yours is marketing and the product I send to your list is about photography chances are not very good that many of them will be interested in a photography product.

But imagine if your product was on marketing and my field of expertise was starting an online business chances would be very good that a lot of your list would be interested in what I'm offering.

Understanding those little nuisances can make the difference between success and failure when it comes to making money online. But don't worry about any of that right now that will be included in your gaining knowledge sections.

Something else I want to share with you here is how do you build a list. Well there are a number of ways to do that the most common is having query boxes on your website and then sending traffic to your site.

Every time someone enters their name and email address in those boxes they will become subscribers to your site and your list. Now what does that really mean for you? It means you have given enough value to that subscriber that he or she wants to know more.

It's your job to give them more but WARNING... Never and I mean never try and sell your product or services up front without first giving value. That's simply not the way your online business will grow the way you want it to.

Once you have your system set up correctly when someone registers with your site you'll have what's called an auto responder to take over at that point. Something else I want you to remember here is to think in terms of 7 points of contact.

What is 7 points of contact you ask well think about when you view a website or read an email or even watch a video each of those is an avenue or point of contact for you to learn what someone does and how what they do can help you.

Now again once your system is set up correctly you will have in place an auto responder and when someone subscribes to your site or email list they should receive a (thank you) email immediately. Consider that the second point of contact.

Here's a (TIP)... Never offer any products or services (for sale) in points of contacts 1 thru 6.

Your objective there is to give something to the prospective subscriber (for free) something of value something such as information a video, an eBook, and there are a host of other items you can use be creative.

The mindset I suggest you use when setting up your individual email campaign is I want to tease my potential subscriber with first class information on what I do and how I could help their situation.

And yes, you will create your own email campaign each and every one it's not difficult at all the only thing to remember is once you have everything in place the way you want it and the way you want your subscriber to view it you have to remember to publish it.

Many people have a problem with that…

However, there is a (preview) prompt that you can click to see what it would look like, prior to publishing but I prefer to publish it then send a test email to my own email address that way I can be sure that my auto responder is working properly.

Again this is where you get to use your creativity because you have the ability to use text, audios, videos, links to podcast and a list of others, all that to share your valuable information and help your future subscriber make up their mind once they've reached that point of contact number 7.

"The challenge is trying to set people free, and help them be 'successful' in the world, which are almost always opposite objectives."

— *Bryant McGill*

Because that's where you'll want to have a product or two that your subscriber can purchase to more increase their knowledge or skill level pertaining to what they do. See how that actually works let me give you a sample walk through of what your auto responder should do once you have everything in place.

Point of contact number one once they subscribe it goes out immediately and it's basically a (thank you) email (nothing) for sale.

Point of contact number two goes out 2 days later. This is where you share information in the form of text.

Point of contact number three goes out 3 days later than that. Again information in the form of text and perhaps a short audio if you have one if not text is fine just make sure it gives value.

Point of contact number four goes out 3 days later than that. In this email you can get a little more creative in the form of using a video if you have one. Remember always thinking about giving value to the subscriber.

Point of contact number five goes out 2 days later than that. By now your new subscriber knows who you are, what you do, and they can identify what you look like. Keep in mind people buy from those they know like and trust.

And if up to this point you've been delivering valuable information tools and techniques that have really moved the needle when it come to their knowledge level or quickened the pace that they were on you've done your job.

Point of contact number six goes out 2 days later. Now you haven't done anything else since you created each email in the campaign and published it everything is done automatically once you do that. From that point on if you get 5 people to subscribe or 5000 people to subscribe your auto responder sends each one the same series of emails.

Finally point of contact number seven goes out 1 day later. In this email you'll want your products or services that you offer to be seen and understood clearly so that your subscriber can purchase right there.

That will require you to have a (checkout process) for your subscribers and make it as simple a process as possible. Because the confused mind always says what (No), right?

Now I trust you could follow along with that process right let me share something else with you that you may or may not know a business is nothing more than a series of systems designed to produce a specific outcome. Which means if you set it up correctly you can put someone else in that position and get the same or better results as if you were doing it yourself.

Just think about your job the people who created your job probably aren't even in the building and they get the same or maybe even better results as if they were there and all they have to do is pay you a fee or wage and you agree to be there for a certain number of hours. It's where you trade money for time your time.

Let me take a little break from the business part of my book right here to share with you something that will become very impactful for you while growing your business. As a God fearing man I enjoy sharing what I call (my 2 cents) on a variety of topics, as well as just giving another perspective to a particular subject.

So, with I'm somewhat of a story teller as a speaker and whenever I get the chance I like to take people down a mental path from time to time. So, if you will now (come with me) and let me open your mind to a different perspective.

We all pray to a God a God who created the universe and everything in it including us. He created everything for a specific purpose we don't know that purpose and never will however, we are part of that purpose each one of us.

What we do while were here matters and is in line with his purpose for us. Now with over 7 billion people on the planet it may be difficult for everyone to identify what their individual purpose is but rest assured they have one.

Our God is so good that not only did he give us a purpose but he also gave us a passion. And once you're able to identify your passion I believe that will lead to your purpose.

Have I lost you yet?

Great well I'm going to go a little deeper. Identifying your passion isn't always easy some people are very good at several things and from the (viewer perspective) i.e. the coach, the dad, the sibling, teacher, etc… they may try and convince you that your passion is that something that you're good at.

You too may enjoy it and you may be so good that you're able to generate a little money or sponsorship for doing it. But that doesn't necessarily mean that's what your passion is.

Only you'll know and a couple of ways to help you decide are: when you're doing something and time seems to pass very quickly but that doesn't seem to matter to you or when you've been doing a particular thing all day and it's late at night and you have to get some rest or you have to get some sleep so you stop and go to bed and while lying in bed your mind says I can't wait to get back to that particular thing those are little indicators for you to consider.

Identifying your passion is only the first step to actually living the life that you want.

Once you do that the next step is becoming an expert at your passion now if your passion is football and you're 40 years old you're not going to play football on most teams but what you can do is begin to share information about football in the form of products that you create.

Now with that I'm going to Segway back to our creator remember he created us in his image.

And for you to become as successful as you want only depends on three steps first gain the knowledge to become an expert.

Second create products based on that knowledge you've gained in the form of audios, videos, books, eBooks, and a host of others.

Third and perhaps most important is to act on the knowledge that you've gained. That's it, it's really that simple the difficult part is to do it.

What you're actually doing is (creating) the life and lifestyle that you want.

Just like the creator who created the entire universe you too are supposed to create your entire universe and life based in part on the passion that you've been given which makes it much easier more fun more rewarding and you've probably heard it said when you working within your passion it's like you're not working at all because you love it.

Today the internet has made it possible for people just like (you) and (me) to go from being totally computer illiterate to starting a business from the comfort of our own home and at our own pace. Also, to become the entrepreneur that we've always wanted to be doing what we love and creating the life we want.

Ok now I have a short test that's right I have a short test for you pertaining to that short story…

1. My objective with that story was to get you to see yourself as _____.

A. Businessman---B. Creator---C. Your own person?

2. Three other products you could also create from that process are _____.

A. Teleseminars, B. Webinars, C. Speaking events, D. Sponsorship programs, E. all of the above?

3. As a creator you'll be creating multiple products which will give you_____.

A. Experience, B. Knowledge, C. Money, D. Multiple Streams of income, E. all of the above?

How'd you like that short test? Kind of cool right!!!

You see as a creator I can put anything in my book that I want to just like you.

The answer to the questions are 1. B- Creator 2. E- All the above 3. E- All of the above.

Now you may not think that you're a writer, well neither did I but today in only a short 5 years I have been able to write 9 books have over 500 videos on YouTube and my own podcast show called SpeakwithLarry's Podcast and those have helped me to not only become better at writing but have also allowed me the opportunity to enjoy doing what I do. Because as creators and inventors of our own business we want that to be in line with what we enjoy doing…right…

"The true asset before any human being on this planet are... Enthusiasm & Will... with these everything comes from nothingness & devoid of them everything perishes to nothingness...

— Dinesh Kumar

Chapter Two: Tools of the Trade…

"A straightforward answer to a straightforward question will move you that much more forward in this world, that much faster."

— *Loren Weisman*

You know how important it is for a professional to have the necessary tools to perform the tasks they do efficiently are right. Well you're not a professional yet but you're working in that direction the great part about that is you get to learn what each part you need will do in real time. The beauty of that is when the time comes to outsource a certain job or skill you know exactly what to expect from the people you outsource it to.

My company boasts about you being able to start your online business with only a phone and a computer and I stick to that however the way technology is advancing soon all you'll need is a phone.

Something else I want you to keep in mind is this is the beginning level one the bottom floor any way you want to say it. So, don't consume your thoughts with trying to get all top of the line tools you'll use right now.

Remember this is a process and just like any other process it will take time. Your objective here is to gain the knowledge about all the tools of the trade you will use for your particular business.

Now as I said earlier this is an internet business an online business and the more familiar you are with surfing the net, googling, emailing, and a host of other terms the faster you'll begin to maneuver from place to place online. So getting better with computers is a must and all that's necessary for you to do that is to practice, practice, practice.

Remember the mindset for you at this point is to focus on becoming an expert at your chosen field and I suggest that whatever that is that it's in line with your passion. Because your passion is something you already like and you won't hate having to spend so much time doing.

This list is dependent on the level you want to reach but these items can be purchased as you grow.

1. Computer
2. Phone
3. Audio Recorder
4. Video Camcorder
5. Printer
6. Video Camera
7. Headsets

8. Microphone
9. Video lights

Now there will be more or less depending on your area of expertise but you can get them at your own pace as you begin to grow.

Another (Tip)…One of the things I've noticed about new people in the business world is they think in order for them to move forward it's necessary that they know everything about each of the new areas they enter.

Not true…for instance there are many things available to do on the computer that you will (never) need to learn the only parts you need to learn will have to do with your business and its functions.

Same goes with the phone, recorders, camcorders, and so on. You always hear people say "If I can do it anyone can" well they are absolutely correct it's that simple.

You simply must make an agreement with yourself that first you will start and second you won't stop until you've become an expert in that area that (you) select.

Success in business just like anything else is not a one man show it takes a team a team that you put together and nurture to get the results that you want.

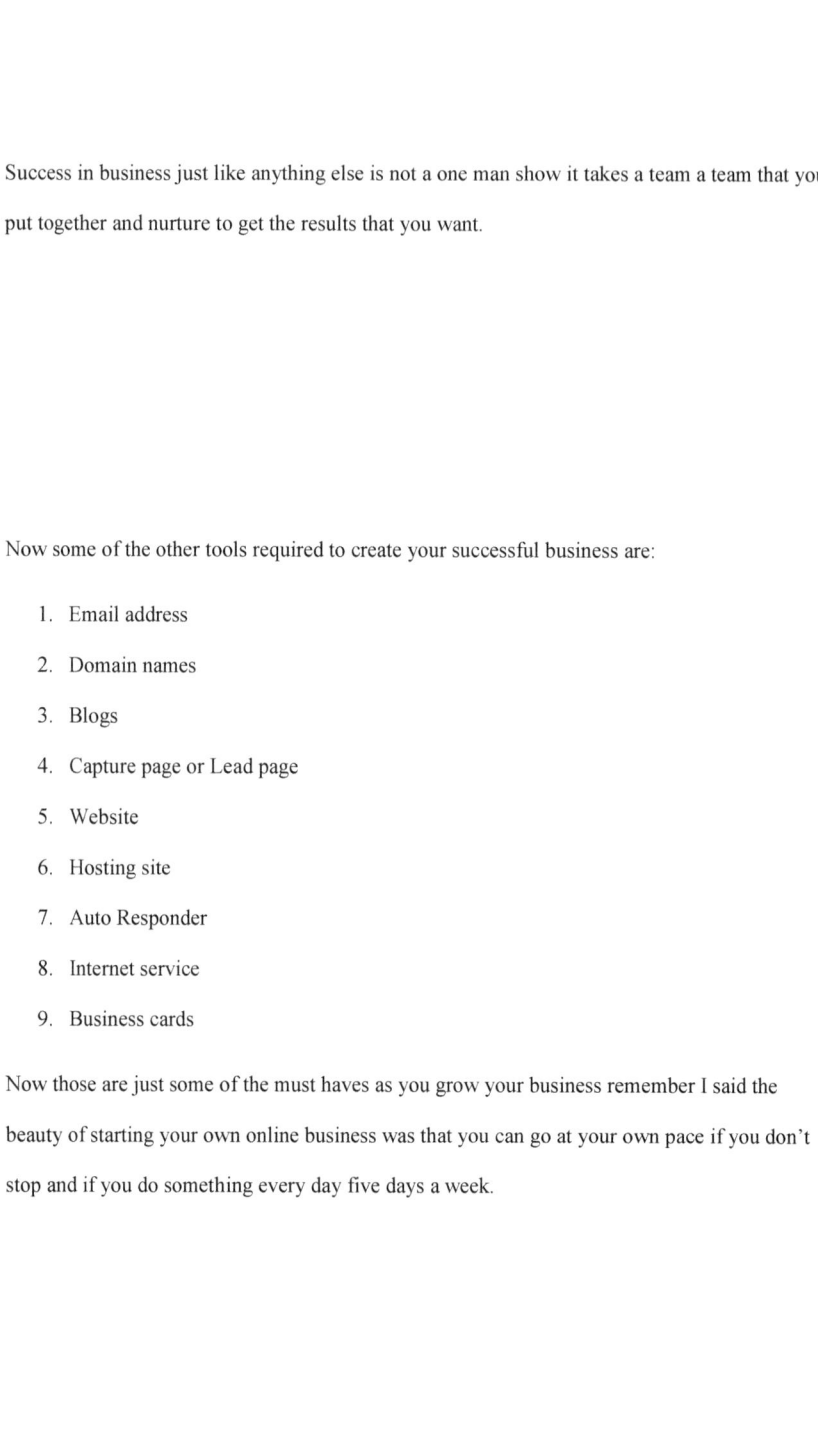

Now some of the other tools required to create your successful business are:

1. Email address
2. Domain names
3. Blogs
4. Capture page or Lead page
5. Website
6. Hosting site
7. Auto Responder
8. Internet service
9. Business cards

Now those are just some of the must haves as you grow your business remember I said the beauty of starting your own online business was that you can go at your own pace if you don't stop and if you do something every day five days a week.

"Never admit more than you have to."

— *Nyrae Dawn*

The mindset I want you to incorporate in the beginning is that of (repetition) that's right think in terms of the fact that you're going to be doing things over and over to get good in an effort to get better and finally in an effort to become an expert at what you do.

And you and I both know that's exactly the way it works in the real world you don't go from (beginner) to (expert) over night. It takes time it takes commitment it takes dedication and those who make it will testify that it was worth every failure every situation circumstance or problem they had to overcome to achieve it.

Let me share something else with you that will benefit you or help grow your business and that's being decisive as you study and gain knowledge about what you're doing don't be hesitant in your decision-making processes.

(For example)

If I asked you what you wanted to name your company would you know?

What about if I asked you the first product you wanted to create would you know?

If I asked you the top 3 places you will market your company to would you know?

If I asked the time of day you will spend time with your business would you know?

And finally, if I asked you the first book you'll read about your business would you know?

You see these are just some of the questions that must be answered and answered by you.

Because from day one you are the CEO, the Owner, the President, and any other adjective you can think of and you must learn all the moving parts associated with your business.

Again the (bonus) for you is that you get to select what that business will be and it will be in line with what you already like what you already enjoy or perhaps even what you already love. How cool is that!!!

Another tool that will serve you well is that of (organization). If you're naturally an organized person this system will fit, you perfectly however if you're somewhat challenged when it comes to organization you may want to consider outsourcing certain duties out to others as soon as you learn and understand how they work.

That's not a good thing or bad thing it's simply recognizing where you're weak and implementing someone else to handle that task or skill. It's also smart because it frees up time for you to do other things that you are good at.

We all know that time is one of our most precious resources and if we can create a system or process that allows us to hire someone else to do a specific thing that would normally take us 3 or 4 hours to do and possibly with several errors it makes total sense to hire them right.

I told you earlier that I love speaking because I love the story telling process. Growing up many children were read to in bed as they prepared to go to sleep. Oftentimes it was the actual reading that put them to sleep. The sound of the voice along with them lying down and quietly listening to their mother or father read two perhaps three pages of a short story that would become ingrained in their subconscious mind and stored.

The benefit of that process wasn't only to put them to sleep but also to allow them to remember the story that was read. Therefore, because of that process when they hear the phrase I'm going to tell you a little story they automatically get still and quiet to hear and understand it.

There are many things involved with how and why we do certain things and many of them have to do with planting things in our subconscious minds.

One of my favorite quotes say "he who is best informed makes the best decisions."

Well to me that's correct because in this life those who are highly educated can pretty much write their own ticket in life. But not everyone has the resources to attend a prestigious university or the knowledge to be accepted into a Harvard or Yale.

But the internet has made it possible for individuals who wouldn't normally be able to receive An Associate's degree, a Bachelors degree, and yes even Masters Degrees to do it from the comfort of their own home and in far less time.

Well, guess what it has also made it possible for people who don't have the resources or the knowledge to start their own online business that's right from the comfort of their own home and yes in far less time.

Now I'm going to give you a word and this word will make you more successful than any other in the world if you simply apply it to as many things as you possibly can and that word is (share).

That's right (share) let me paint a picture for you right here let's say you wrote a poem and everyone you read it to absolutely loved it they raved about it. Now the reason they loved it and was able to rave about it was you shared it with them.

So let's take it to the next level let's say you created a CD with that very same poem and begin to market it in a different way to a different group of people and you got the same results they loved it.

What happens after that is you create a video with that same poem and make it available to a different group of people and before you know it your sales from that one poem has increase so much that it's allowed you to pay some things off and upgrade your materials.

Now do you stop no you continue creating more poems and process them through that same funnel that you used for the first poem. First of all you've created name recognition and whenever your stuff comes out people automatically want it.

Second you've created value because what was in your poem others were able to see and share with their people through their understand and Third you've increased your skills and understanding of the entire process.

Now that one word (share) has allowed you to do all of those things simply because you chose to share it rather than keep in in your note pad or computer or even worst in your mind.

Now I'm going to give you some of the avenues you'll want to consider when setting up your multiple streams of income for your business. You're free to choose one, two, three, or as many as you like.

1. Writing eBooks
2. Writing Books
3. Creating Audio Programs (CD's)

4. Creating Video Programs (DVD's)
5. Speaking (Motivational) (Keynote)
6. Tele-Seminars
7. Webinars
8. Podcast
9. Sponsorship

Now there's more I just wanted you to get a taste of some of the options available to people just like you and I who are not computer geniuses and don't have a ton of money or free time. As you can see the time for (excuses) no longer apply so all you need to do from this point on is to make the decision that you're ready to start and let's get the ball rolling.

"Clutter is the physical manifestation of unmade decisions fueled by procrastination"
― *Christina Scalise*

Chapter Three: Identifying Your Passion…

"The saddest people I've ever met in life are the ones who don't care deeply about anything at all. Passion and satisfaction go hand in hand, and without them, any happiness is only temporary, because there's nothing to make it last."

— *Nicholas Sparks*

I've been teaching on this subject for the past 3 years and for some reason most people I speak with say they don't really know what their passion is are you one of those?

A lot of people say I know I want to help people or I want to do something with children and the list goes on. But I say to them you need to be more specific when you say you want to help people that could mean feeding the homeless or collecting clothing for the elderly or even working with meals on wheels.

And that list could go on for quite a while. While you say, you want to do something with children do you mean work as a day care provider work as a school crossing guard or be an elementary school teacher.

You get the point right!!!

The identifying your passion I'm talking about is specific things like photography, bowling, art, golf, poetry, music, and the list goes on. The reason it needs to be specific is that you'll be teaching it and you'll be teaching it in a variety of formats or platforms. Things like writing about it in blogs, articles, posts, and so on.

The key word in identifying your passion is (your) it is specific to you and no one else. Keep in mind when I say no one else I don't mean no one else has that same passion what I mean is only you will know for sure what your passion is.

Let me tell you a short story about how I was able to identify my passion.

Some years ago, 15 or 20 I wanted to become a real-estate investor and I have always known that you must gain the knowledge before you can play the game. I had no problem with that I'm a good student and was very eager to learn.

Gaining the knowledge I needed required that I attend seminars and listen to different people talk about real estate. Now as I'm listening to these speaker's I'm imagining that it was me on stage giving those crowd moving speeches traveling from city to city and collecting those large speaking fees for a one hour keynote. It all sounded very enticing to me.

But wait I had never spoken to a crowd of people before however in my mind I thought well how hard could it be?

Well it was a lot harder than I thought but guess what it wasn't the process that was hard it was the fact that I found out I had a fear of speaking in public.

Who knew right I surely didn't.

Now I'm the type of person who loves to gain knowledge or learn something that I didn't know. And I had read several books that said "Everything you want is right on the other side of what you fear." Or they would say something like "You can have anything you want but you have to take action".

I kept hearing all those types of things in the back of my mind so I decided to do something about it and I joined Toastmasters. That's an organization that helps you with understanding moves, gestures, mannerisms, and a lot of other things that go with public speaking.

After about a month I realized just how much I really didn't know or understood about speaking but more than that I realized just how fearful I was of it.

Now keep in mind I love the concept of being paid to come and speak about a certain topic and traveling around the world on their dime so to speak I love that but I needed to find a way to overcome my fear of speaking in front of an audience.

Because you know when you fear something you'll psychologically put up roadblocks in order to avoid doing it. Well so did I but I knew without a doubt that was what I needed to overcome.

Now I'm not saying you'll fear your passion I'm simply saying that's the way it happened for me.

So I plotted a little events schedule to attend and watch more speakers speak in order to pick up styles and techniques and before long I was pretty familiar with the way the speaking business really worked.

This is one of the (takeaways) I want you to get because it's very important and can cut down on some of the time you'll have to invest. And that's learn exactly the way the industry works the one you're choosing to become a part of.

(For example)

If you're going to create an eBook, you need to know where you're going to write it in Microsoft Word are you going to type it and transfer it into Microsoft word or some other place then you'll want to know once you've finished who's going to proof read it or even if you want it proof read.

Next, you'll need to know who's going to publish it then you'll want to know how you're going to market it and finally you need to know where you are going to sell it. See how that works…

So, what I did was set up a way for me to become knowledgeable about my topic or what would eventually become my business. My company teaches you how to set up the foundation of your online business while helping you become more comfortable speaking about it.

In the online business world, you're either creating products or services and once you've determined which you'll do next comes the magic.

"Passion is a feeling that tells you: this is the right thing to do. Nothing can stand in my way. It doesn't matter what anyone else says. This feeling is so good that it cannot be ignored. I'm going to follow my bliss and act upon this glorious sensation of joy."
— *Wayne W. Dyer*

I set out on a mission to create products my first product was a paperback book titled "Your New Boss looks like this; can you trust them." After that came another book titled "You the most Valuable piece to your Success."

Shortly after that came my first CD then another CD then another. The next progression for me was videos while doing videos I discovered something else about myself I love creating videos.

I love being in front of the camera and sharing information with the world I love it some much that today I have well over 700 videos online and I continue to make them every chance I get.

But guess what creating those videos allowed me to watch myself after I record them and critic myself and consequently I've gotten better speaking.

Isn't that amazing today I'm marketing myself as someone who went from having a fear of speaking in public to someone who became sought after to speak.

Now from time to time when I get on stage I still feel the gitters but nowhere near as when I began.

And the one thing I've learned along my journey is that everything is a process in the beginning you're not going to be very good but if you don't stop you'll get better and sometimes you become the best.

Something else I want to share with you about identifying your passion and that's you can have more than one passion. Many times, while doing something that you really enjoy that can open a door to another opportunity that you had no idea you liked. But you come to find out that you not only like it but you love it.

Now when you do what you love and get paid for it you can become a master at it.

Kind of like I told you earlier about me liking to speak but as I did more speaking I realized I enjoyed creating videos.

So as you're thinking about your passion keep in mind that you can start doing something in one area and end up doing something totally different. Just be mindful that you're going to create a business around the knowledge you gain about what you decide your passion is. So ask yourself what would you like to learn about?

When you're preparing yourself to learn enough about your passion or in this case your business to become an expert it's necessary that you focus on 3 things these 3 things I teach and that's Belief, Knowledge, and Accountability.

Many of the people I help set up the foundation of their businesses lack a certain level of belief in themselves at least initially. And by increasing their knowledge about the business they want to start that increases their belief in themselves.

Now piggyback that with holding them accountable by helping the set and reach a series of short term goals, goals that are in line with what they want to be, do and have, and that also increases their belief in themselves.

Now you may be asking yourself why am I focusing so much on belief in yourself right here?

Well it's because this is the foundation and belief in you is a must right here. Because if you don't believe in you if you don't believe it's possible for you and you don't believe you deserve it guess what you'll never get it.

First, the minute you decide to do something different others will automatically begin to say negative things about you and to you.

Which is why I know knowledge about something allows you to see things those without that knowledge can't see.

So, say it with me the three elements of setting up a solid foundation are Belief, Knowledge, and Accountability.

The next thing I want to discuss with you are levels many of us once we decide we want to do a certain something we want to go from level one to level ten overnight.

Well sorry but that's not quite the way it works you must get some bumps and bruises along the journey.

The example I like to use about levels is; imagine today that you won the lottery. Let's say 10 million dollars think about for a moment really process it…you've won 10million dollars.

There are a series of things you'll do first, second, third, and so on, most of those will have very little to do with your needs and more to do with your wants right…

The first thing that probably hasn't really resonated with you just yet is you're no longer on the same level.

That's right you actually did go from level one to level ten overnight.

Now what do you do?

You see now its real time this isn't monopoly money its real money yours.

How do you handle it, who do you trust, how do you invest, where do you put 10 million dollars?

These are questions that must be answered now!

Fortunately, most people never have to deal with this situation but, many would love the opportunity.

Perhaps you're one of those!!!

The way most of us do it is we go from level one to level two, three, four and so on, which is great also and it gives you several other benefits that overnight success can't possibly give you.

- You get to learn at your own pace.
- The mistakes you make aren't quite as costly.
- As you grow you get to understand the way it makes you feel.
- You create valuable contacts those you've grown to know like and trust.
- Fifth and finally the most important in my opinion is you know the person you've become.

You've made some mistakes and overcome them you've had successes and stayed humble and trust me once you've reached the highest level possible in your area of expertise everything that you've accomplished the awards, the material possession, the money, all of it pales in comparison to who you've become.

"Politeness is okay, but it gets old and boring. You want to attack life with a passion, not a politeness, you want people to think about you and remember you and say "she is so passionate" you don't want people to think about you and remember you and say "she is so polite," because, who cares about polite?"

— C. JoyBell C.

Chapter Four: Setting up your work area…

"Choose a job you love, and you will never have to work a day in your life."

― *Confucius*

This may not be an issue for you but for many it is. When you decide to start a business, you must take every aspect of it very seriously even setting up your work area. If your resources are limited from the beginning which many people do have limited resources at first try and set aside an area that you can go to everyday to work on your business, then upgrade as you're able to.

Some of the things you'll probably need to keep on hand at all times are:

- Staples
- Pens
- Printer Ink
- Note Pads
- Letter Opener
- White Out
- Markers
- Printer Paper
- Double A and triple A
- Stick Notes

- Envelopes
- Stapler

Now there will be more or less depending on your particular business or niche. The mindset necessary here is when they get low simply focus on replacing them.

Now once you've set your work area up and have decided on the schedule you'll work your next objective is to become an expert on your business. You'll read books, listen to audios, watch videos, and other avenues to gain knowledge on your business because you want to become an expert in your area.

I created a "Set up your foundation in 90 days" process that included only 3 books and the Internet. What it did was allow you to gain the knowledge necessary to become an expert in your field.

And this is the way it worked once you decided on the business you wanted to start go out and buy 3 books on that subject.

Set up a schedule to read one books per month (cover to cover) no exceptions on this one. You want to read one book per month. After you've read the first chapter of book number one go to YouTube and type in (your business) let's say its photography type that in and they'll have all types of videos for you to watch that will teach and guide you to other places to learn more about your niche.

Set up a schedule to watch at least 5 videos per day 3 days per week. After you've watched videos for one week go back on line and register with two sites that are in line with your business. They'll begin to send you more information and any updates that are taking place in your business.

Now after reading, watching videos, listening to audios, listening to podcast and a list of other platforms your level of expertise will increase very fast.

And at the end of 90 days imagine I'm going to come to you and ask you 3 questions about your business. You won't know the questions that I'm going to ask all you'll know is that there's going to be 3 questions could you answer?

Let me ask you if you walked into a doctor's office today and asked them 3 questions about their profession could they answer?

What about a lawyer? If you walked into a tax lawyer's office today and asked them 3 questions about taxes could they answer?

Well my answer would be Yes, yes, they could and so will you only in much less time.

Finally in this chapter I want to share with you some of the benefits of starting a business today.

Now the process that got me here was first I wrote a book but you don't know anything about writing a book right I get that.

Neither did I and if you ever get a chance to read my first book you probably would agree with me but that didn't stop me.

Because I believe that we all have at least one book in us. And over the past 5 years I know that to be a fact because if I get a pen and pad and sit down with you and ask you a series of questions I can create a short eBook just from the information that you give me.

But beyond that let me share something else you that you may not know after I finished writing my book and had it published I thought the hard part was over... not.

You see I knew nothing about marketing, but not only did I know nothing about it I didn't know I needed to.

Now you may laugh but you may have a testimonial of your own.

So, fast forward till today and every product I create I create knowing how I'm going to market it.

Let me say one more thing about marketing before I move on starting out many times because of finances you must do all the marketing yourself and that's ok just be mindful that at some point it will probably make more sense to outsource that skill to people who are more versed at that than you are.

Ok, now thanks to the internet the world of starting a business has changed dramatically and when I say dramatically no longer does it take a credit score of 800, or a brick and mortar location, it doesn't even require that you have a large start up cash flow.

All that's needed for you to start your own business today is a phone, a computer and "BAM" you're in business. And the way technology is advancing soon all you'll need is a phone.

During my journey as an online business owner I've had the obligation of wearing many different hats and before it's over so will you. That's always part of the growth process because the more you know and understand about all the moving parts of your business the better.

Today as an entrepreneur there are a number of ways to monetize your skills and abilities. And as you gain more knowledge about your business I suggest you incorporate as many of them into your system as you can effectively.

"The human race is a monotonous affair. Most people spend the greatest part of their time working in order to live, and what little freedom remains so fills them with fear that they seek out any and every means to be rid of it."

— *Johann Wolfgang von Goethe*

Chapter Five: Creating Your Products…

"If you keep your eye on the profit, you're going to skimp on the product. But if you focus on making really great products, then the profits will follow."

— *Steve Jobs*

Alright, this is where the fun begins for you I know you've been busy studying and gaining knowledge about your business and now you're ready to act on all that you've learned.

I spoke earlier in the book about you looking at yourself as a creator well this is where you get to take some of the things in your head and share them with the world in the form of your products.

Your first question may be what product do I create first? That's a fair question my short answer would be what do you enjoy more? Do you enjoy the idea of creating audios, videos, or writing because if you enjoy writing more you can start with an eBook or maybe just a regular paperback it's all up to you?

All the clients I help with this process I make sure they know that anything you do for the first time you're probably not going to be really good at so don't lose enthusiasm if it takes a little longer than you plan and don't get frustrated when you find several mistakes or errors in your first product.

Because just like anything else if you don't stop you will get better and remember you're going to create several products so just enjoy the process.

The mindset I keep when creating my products is I want to know enough about everything so that I could teach it to someone else once I finish. You can feel free to incorporate that in your process as well.

Now I want to talk to you about the differences between creating some of these products. When you write an eBook, the process is going to be different than creating a CD or video. However, they all have one thing in common and that's you must have written a script or in the case of the eBook you may want to call it a rough draft.

I've created several CD's and even a series of CD's designed to help you set up the foundation of your online business and once you've written your script and you begin recording it you will have to make correction as you go that's just the way it works even if you think everything is perfect trust me you will need to make adjustments.

A few other things you'll want to focus on after you've decided on the product you'll create is the title and the length of your creation. Selecting a great title is a definite advantage for your product because like a headline if it's interesting enough it will make the viewer want to look inside or listen to what's inside.

And when I talk about the length of your CD, Video, eBook, or Book you'll want to take into consideration your listeners or readers attention span. Think about yourself when you go to buy a book or CD what's your evaluating process?

Are you interested in listening to a 45 minute CD about what you like or would you rather it be at least an hour long? Then ask yourself would you rather read an eBook with 50 pages or one with 100 pages?

Keep in mind you too are a consumer and other people market their products to you as well.

Now so far, I've only covered a few things involving creating your products but even with that you should be able see just how hands on this process will be for you. Which is why one of the benefits of creating your products is you get to go at your own pace.

But remember from start to finish is not an open-ended process and you should have a schedule and deadline to complete your project but you're able to be flexible in the process.

The way I do it is I like creating my products in a quarter in a 4-month period I like to go from writing the entire script or manuscript to sending the finished product to my publisher.

You may be able to finish in less time that's great but again you get to go at your own pace and if it takes longer than the 4 months you can actually see where you went wrong or if you need to work on committing more to your projects.

My system allows you to begin, monitor, and adjust any aspect of creating your products. That's exactly the type of control you'll want over all your products.

I want to talk with you for a moment about writing your scripts and manuscripts. As you're studying and learning as much as you can about your business always remember to take notes.

When you take notes put them in a place where you can get to them as you need to because when you're writing you may have just the quote or lesson you want to share but you're not exactly sure of the correct wording having your notes in a place that you can get to them makes the process a lot easier.

Something else I want to reiterate businesses are nothing more than a series of systems designed to create a desired result. Once you understand the process of writing a book, creating a CD, or a host of other products you have the ability to create as many as you like whenever you like how cool is that right…

One of things I tell people who are struggling with staying focused is from time to time you will lose focus so think back to your (why). Why did you want to start your own business? Understanding your why has the ability to get you up when you need that little boost.

As I work on gaining knowledge about the things I have to learn, I get the opportunity to learn from some of the real key players or key figures in my industry. One of the guys I've studied in the past is named Jon Mroz and he shared with me the best example of (understanding your why) that I've ever heard, and I want to share that with you today.

Now I want you to mentally walk down this path with me if you will; if you could visually imagine that I have a plank and the plank is 30 feet long and 10 inches wide picture those dimensions in your head before I continue got it good.

So, I say to you I'm going to place this plank on the ground and if you walk from one end to the other I'll give you $20 dollars would you do it?

Probably so right, that's a quick $20 dollars, isn't it?

Well imagine that I take that same plank and place it between two buildings 25 stories tall as a bridge and offered you that same $20 dollars to walk from one end to the other would you do it? Probably not right…

Well imagine that one of the buildings was on fire and your child was on top of that building, would you walk across then?

Absolutely! Right!!! I wouldn't even have to give you the $20 dollars would I?

That's how bad you need to want your business to succeed everything is dependent on you just like your child's life depended totally on you saving them everything within your business is dependent on you to make it work.

"Create a link through which you can market your dream products. Create a blog or a website of your own depending on what you want to be recognized for. Share your experiences through these media."

― *Israelmore Ayivor*

Chapter Six: Three things to work on daily…

"People tend to be generous when sharing their nonsense, fear, and ignorance. And while they seem quite eager to feed you their negativity, please remember that sometimes the diet we need to be on is a spiritual and emotional one. Be cautious with what you feed your mind and soul. Fuel yourself with positivity and let that fuel propel you into positive action."

― *Steve Maraboli*,

This is one of my favorite chapters because there's so much growth that can come from positioning each of these as a priority in your life. It took me quite a while to actually understand just how important feeding these three things on a daily basis was.

Now I don't go a day without adding in some way to each of them and I mean 7 days a week.

Do you know what those are? Take a guess…well if you said the Mind, Body, and Spirit you'd be correct.

As you decide on the way you want to work on your mind the simplest way to do that is to learn something about your business every day.

When it comes to your body that will depend on a few things first how do you look now are you fit do you currently work out? If the answer to that is (no) then you'll need to start slowly because too much of a change will cause you to either stop or not enjoy what you're doing. Which will eventually cause you to stop.

Now the spirit which I believe is the easiest to implement because we all believe in our God and if you only read a paragraph or a section of a daily bread you've accomplished all that's necessary to complete the three.

Next I want to share with (why) it's good to incorporate ways to add to these three every day.

First, you've probably heard it said that success is not a good teacher right well that's true. Something that must be taken into consideration when you think about having success is you're either going to remain humble or you're going to let the success make you another type of person.

Success in this situation can be interchangeable with money.

Because when you give some people money it will expose some very telling signs about their character. Keep in mind that those people were probably that way already it was just the money that brought it out. Well guess what success will do the same thing.

On the flip side of that failure is a different beast. It has the ability to lower a person's self-esteem and make them feel worthless. But most detrimental to your growth and success failure has the ability to make you quit make you stop and make you give up.

However, unlike success failure is an excellent teacher. When you experience failure at anything, you have the opportunity to reassess the situation looking at the way you did something or the way you responded to something and learn from it and try again (only wiser).

As you're deciding on the different ways you'll add to your mind, body, and spirit some other words you'll want to incorporate into your system are commitment, consistency, and perseverance.

Because regardless of what you're doing in life those three words if applied together will garner the results that you seek.

Nothing can ever be accomplished if you're not willing to make the commitment to go through the entire process of acquiring what you want. If you want a college degree and you're fortunate enough to have the funding in place to attend college if you don't go to class guess what you can't receive a degree.

You must go through the entire process what does that mean it means there will be times when you don't feel like going to class there will be times when someone in your life will become ill there will be times when your car will break down and the list goes on.

You simply have to as they say (man up) and get through it. If for whatever reason you decide to quit or stop going the possibility of you receiving that degree becomes less and less.

When you think about the way life really works it's all about choices a guy once asked me do you know what the fastest way to become successful is? I said no what he said to finish what you start. Now that sounds simple enough right but many of us seem to overload our proverbial plates and before you know it we're leaving a lot of things unfinished.

About 10 years ago I had the privilege of attending a speaking event in Dallas Texas and the keynote speaker that day was a guy by the name of Jack Canfield. He was fantastic that day but before he left he said somethings that really stayed with me and I'm going to share a few of those with you here today and hopefully you can incorporate some into your system.

Now this isn't going to be verbatim or exactly the way he said it and remember it was 10 years ago, but he said when you agree to do something for someone else or you decide to do something for yourself and don't follow through or finish what you started what happens is that that registers in your mind as an (incomplete).

And when you've registered enough incompletes they begin to translate (in your mind) as failures. That made a lot of sense to me and once you get comfortable not completing what you start you'll tend to make that (ok for yourself) not finishing what you commit to.

Something else I remember him talking about that day he said take an assessment of your surroundings your car, your home, your work environment, and any other place you spend time, and if something is not working either fix it or throw it away.

Now that may be difficult for some of you to understand or agree with but when you think about it when something is occupying space and it's not working it's taking up valuable space to put something that does work.

It also de clutters your mind because let's say you needed a new printer and you have the finances to purchase one but you have so many items in your home or office that don't work but you are reluctant to throw them away and in your mind the question arises where do I put it?

Well that's the way we process things in our life too perhaps you've heard the phrase, "the confused mind always says (no)," well that's true. And the cluttered environment always leads to stagnation.

Now another of my favorite words is (consistency) very few things are ever achieved without that word coming into play. The main reason for that is most things require time and for you to get the results you seek in any area will mean certain things must be done and normally over and over.

I have a podcast show I created about 10 months ago, and when I was setting everything up for the show I really knew very little about what I was doing. And through trial and error and perseverance I was able to get all the moving parts in place. But that was only the beginning because I still had to create the individual episodes for the show.

I had to decide if I would create one, two, or three episodes per week, now keep in mind that I do a lot of other things besides create podcast episodes and my time is very valuable for that reason alone.

So I settled on creating one episode each week and on Mondays. Now as of today's date May 11th 2015 I have created 52 episodes. Can you guess one of the words that comes into play in order to create 52 episodes of a podcast show? Absolutely (consistency).

Now after you've made the commitment to what you're going to do then created the systems so that you can repeat the process with some consistency next you must persevere.

What does that look like to you? Well, when you've done your best and put your best foot forward but you don't get the results you seek you must continue.

One of the definitions of persevere says "to continue in a course of action even in the face of difficulty or with little or no prospect of success."

That hits the nail right on the head when it comes to life because as you know there are no guarantees to the outcome of your effort even if you've planned, practiced, prayed, and stayed patient, the results you get may be less than you feel you deserve.

But you can't give up you must continue because if you don't if you don't persevere you'll eliminate any chance you have of accomplishing what you want.

Let me give you a quick example on what it's like to give up on what you want.

This short story was told by a guy named Willie Jolly also a professional motivational speaker. It's about 3 guys who wanted a Coke a Cola.

Imagine its 11o'clock at night and (guy number one) wakes up and decides he wants a coke he looks in the refrigerator and there's not any he goes to the window looks out and it's snowing so he gets a glass of water and goes back to bed. He evidently didn't want it bad enough.

(Guy number two) wakes up and decides he wants a coke he looks in the refrigerator and there aren't any he looks out the window and sees that it's snowing. He puts on his clothes and goes to the store a block away when he gets there the store is closed so he goes back home drinks some orange juice and go back to bed. I guess he didn't want it bad enough either.

Now (guy number three) wakes up and decides he wants a coke looks in the refrigerator and there aren't any he looks out the window and it's snowing. He puts his clothes on and goes and to the corner store and it's closed so he drives about a mile to another store and you guessed it it's closed also so he gets back in the car and drives three miles in the other direction to an outside soda machine and it's sold out. But rather than go back home he continues to drive to another location about 30 minutes away and finally locates a store that's open he goes in and buys a 6 pack of cokes.

That ladies and gentlemen is what perseverance looks like in real time. In other words there will be obstacles, roadblocks, and setbacks, you simply have to continue. Overcoming is what determines whether or not you'll achieve what you seek.

"When you think yours is the only true path you forever chain yourself to judging others and narrow the vision of God. The road to righteousness and arrogance is a parallel road that can intersect each other several times throughout a person's life. It's often hard to recognize one road from another. What makes them different is the road to righteousness is paved with the love of humanity. The road to arrogance is paved with the love of self."

― *Shannon L. Alder*

Chapter Seven: Social Media connections…

"Social media allows us to behave in ways that we are hardwired for in the first place - as humans. We can get frank recommendations from other humans instead of from faceless companies."

― *Francois Gossieaux*

With the discovery of the internet the world as we know it has changed totally. And you can trust this it will never be the same. I told you earlier that my company teaches you how to set up the foundation of your online business while helping you become comfortable speaking about it.

Well for me to teach you to do that you must register with my site online along with many other sites that you're probably already familiar with and some you're probably already registered with.

It's important to realize that the internet has far more options available than you will ever need so don't get intimidated when you're learning how to implement them into your system. I'm going to give you a brief chart of the way I structured my system in the first 90 days so feel free to follow the same path if you like.

The first thing I needed to do was to decide on the type of business I wanted to start and for me it was (business) with a minor in (speaking) if you will. That's because I learned early on that you could quickly increase your opportunities for success if you would just speak about it.

Now that may not be the road you select because many people have a fear of speaking in public. But remember so did I and through trial and error and perseverance I'm a lot better at it and you will get better too if you simply work on it.

So, since I had the first part solid and in place my next step was to register with a couple of sites that was in line with business and speaking. Guess what there we're hundreds.

All that's necessary to register is a short eight or nine question questionnaire things like your (email address) (date of birth) (first and last name) and a few others and like magic you're in. Now the sites you select are totally up to you and you can unsubscribe any time you like.

And you will unsubscribe to some sites from time to time that's only normal.

These are some of the sites you'll want to incorporate into your system keep in mind there will be more or less this is just a beginning list.

1. Facebook
2. Twitter
3. Linked In
4. Google Plus
5. Pinterest
6. Instagram
7. Tumblr
8. Flickr
9. Meetup

Again keep in mind that social media sites are basically a place for you to become known to an audience for the things that you do. Think about if you walked into a room of 50 people and no one knows who you are if you get up in front of the room and introduce yourself and tell everyone in the room what you do you're no longer a stranger. People now know who you are what you do and what you look like.

All that's left is for you to begin to give people (value) that is one of the key words on the internet (value).

Always think in terms of creating (content) that will give your audience (value). And remember you'll create content in several different venues such as articles, blogs, website, audios, videos, and a host of others. Just figure out the one you'll want to do first, second, third, and so on.

For instance one of the things I love to do is share motivational quotes with some of my followers and I do it every day.

The main reason I love sharing quotes is in order for me to decide on which one I will share I have to read it myself and that for me is therapeutic for me as well. And on Facebook is where I have chosen to share my motivational quotes.

On LinkedIn I don't share quotes there I leave comments, start discussions, and I have my setting positioned from my podcast shows to automatically go to LinkedIn each time I create one which I do every Monday.

With Twitter I have my setting set from my other sites to automatically go there with everything I do from audios, videos, posts, and so on.

"Be a person that others will look for your posts daily because they know you will encourage them. Be the positive one and help others to have a great day and you will find that not only they like you but you will like you too."

— *John Patrick Hickey*

Pinterest is a place where I go to look and choose what I want to pin on boards that I create for instance they have a variety of topics that I can look through and if I see a nice car, a suit, or anything I like I simply click on it and like magic it's pinned on my page.

You'll love the amount of different things you can choose from while on that site.

Now I'm not going to go through all the others right now because you'll learn a lot incorporating them into your system but I do want to touch on meetup very quickly.

Meetups are groups put together by an individual or several people design to assist others new and experienced with growing their businesses and one of the beauties of the meetup groups in my opinion is they're specific to what they teach.

For instance, some of the groups help with networking, social media, speaking, and the list goes on. You simply join and you get the benefit of everything they offer.

I studied a lady by the name of Genie Z. LaBorde and she was talking about "How to erase anxiety and boost success." Now this is under the umbrella of (NLP) which is Neuro-linguistic programming.

She talked about what's called the (right brain switch) she says (NLP) is the most elegant way to switch on the capabilities of your right brain. She also states that the reason it's important to tap into the right brain is because the right brain has all the goodies things like peace, joy, creativity, bliss, self-healing, and much more.

Now to contrast that she talks about the (left brain) and says it's full of fear and anxiety.

And there's no fear or anxiety in the (right brain). Therefore, when you make the switch to the right brain anxiety disappears. And consequently, the more often the (right brain) is activated the less fear there will be each time you switch back to the left brain.

The reason I wanted to include this segment here in this chapter was to help you change your mindset and understand exactly what it means when you hear the term (right brain) and (left brain).

Now as a (bonus) I'm going to give you a list of some of the things on the Right and the Left brain.

(Right) brain consists of:

- Peace
- Joy
- Pictures
- Bliss
- Creativity
- Self-Healing
- Now
- Expansiveness One with All
- Parallel Processing Collage All at Once.

Also just imagine the advantage you'll have over those who don't have a clue about the way this actually works.

(Left) brain consists of:

1. Logic
2. Analysis
3. Organization
4. Language

5. Fear
6. Anxiety
7. Past
8. Future
9. Serial Processing in Sequence One at a Time.

"You can't know a person by anything other than being around them personally. This social media can't "capture" humans."

— *Dexsta Ray*

I want you to read each list over several times and try and remember when you're feeling or thinking a certain way you'll be able to identify which side of the brain you're working in at the time. Knowing that will be valuable to you because you can consciously switch when you need to.

Now I'm a student of the mind and I truly feel that knowing certain things will greatly increase your ability to succeed. So, with that I wanted to share this segment title "Your Brain in Action" perhaps you've heard some parts of it or all of it before but I feel that by you knowing it will change your perspective about the way the brain works. Keep in mind knowledge is power…

Your Brain the way it works

Have you ever asked yourself what do I really know about the brain? Well I want you to think about that question for a moment because whether you have or not today I'm going to share some information with you that will clear up some of the things that perhaps have puzzled you from time to time about the brain.

Now I've read several books and watched countless videos on this subject and I'm confident that when you finish this segment you will have a clearer view of how the brain actually works.

And yes, I too have wondered from time to time what goes on and this is the way it was explained to me and I am today sharing it with you.

There are 2 major parts of the brain the (conscious) and the (sub-conscious) or the (subjective) and the (objective). We all know that right! well I heard the best example that anyone I've ever studied has given and it goes like this.

Think of your conscious mind the mind you're using right now to pay attention to me as the captain of a ship and look at your subconscious mind as all the other soldiers on that ship and the only thing they do is follow the instructions that the captain gives them.

Are you with me?

Because that's the relationship that the conscious mind has with the subconscious. Ok, now I'm going to give you some contrasts between the conscious and the subconscious but first let me ask you a question.

Which part of the brain do you believe stores or houses the most information the (conscious) or the (subconscious)?

If you said the subconscious you're absolutely correct. Very good.

Now the conscious mind has been called Volitional which means it sets goals, judge's results, and it likes to try new things. Your conscious mind would be the part of your brain that says let's go sky diving.

Whereas your subconscious mind is called habitual which means it monitors the operations of the body and its motor functions things like the heart rate, blood pressure, digestive system and so on. Now it prefers the familiar so when your conscious mind says let's go sky diving your subconscious mind says (oh no), that's not a good idea.

The main reason for that is you've never done that type of thing before so the subconscious mind has no information to compare it to and remember the subconscious minds job is to keep you safe.

Which makes sense, right!

Another contrast says your conscious mind thinks (abstractly) and it's conceptually based while your subconscious mind thinks (literally) and is sensor based. Which means it sees the world through your five senses taste, touch, smell, and so on.

Also, your conscious mind is known as your short-term memory the average length of a thought is normally about 20 seconds did you know that? But it's also (time bound) meaning it deals with the past and the future.

Whereas your subconscious mind is your long-term memory it stores past experiences, attitudes, values, and beliefs. And it's also considered (timeless) because it deals with the present time only. Did you know that?

The next thing I want to share with you is your conscious mind has a limited processing capacity meaning it can handle only 1 to 3 events or an average of 2000 bits of information per second.

What would that look like well, think about this…if you're listening to a song and a couple of people came in the room and tried to talk to you at the same time your conscious mind would say wait hold on that's too much information at one time.

Whereas your subconscious mind has an expanded processing capacity which can handle thousands of events and an average of 4 billion that's right billion with a B bits of information per second. Incredible right!

Finally, keep in mind that you have 2 hemispheres of the brain the left and the right hemispheres. The left brain deals with logic, words, parts, and when I say parts I mean it likes to break things down into parts to solve them and it also likes order and control.

The right brain deals with emotions, pictures, whole, and when I say whole I mean it likes to look at things from a whole perspective. But most importantly it's easier to change habits of thought and behavior if you access the subconscious mind because it is the storehouse for attitudes, values, and beliefs.

Which will allow you to change the "I can't" messages that you carry around with you like I can't start a business, I can't make any money, and I can't speak in public. To I can accomplish anything I choose, I'm a worthy and valuable person, and I deserve happiness and success in my life.

Now that segment I learned long ago and I like to share it whenever possible that's how important I believe it to be.

"The Net's interactivity gives us powerful new tools for finding information, expressing ourselves, and conversing with others. It also turns us into lab rats constantly pressing levers to get tiny pellets of social or intellectual nourishment."

— *Nicholas Carr,*

Chapter Eight: Marketing and Branding…

"Doing business without advertising is like winking at a girl in the dark. You know what you are doing but nobody else does."

— *Steuart Henderson Britt*

As an entrepreneur these two words will need to become ingrained in your mindset and thought process from day one. I told you earlier when I wrote my first book after I had it finished and published I thought the hard part was over not at all you see I knew nothing about marketing or branding.

Now five years later and several products later every product I create I create knowing how I'm going to market and brand them. And I suggest that if you haven't created a product or started your business yet that you incorporate studying something about marketing and branding also.

Now Wikipedia says, (marketing) is, communicating the value of a product service or brand to customers for promoting or selling that product service or brand.

Something else I want you to understand from the beginning is that you're not starting a business to become a marketer however, you will learn marketing techniques along the way and I recommend that you become as efficient as you possibly can at it but as soon as you begin to generate enough money from the growth of your business I suggest that you outsource that skill to others who are more versed at that than you are.

So why would I suggest that you assign that responsibility to someone else?

Well it's because the business you start will have several different skills that will be needed to make your company successful. And as soon as you're able to master each of those skills your next objective is to identify different companies that you can associate yourself with that you can outsource some of those skills to and pay them a fee.

What that does is it frees up one of your most valuable assets (time) which allows you to spend more time with other things like your family, vacations, children's events, and others, plus you no longer have to spend your valuable time on the maintenance of your business.

I want to share with you a process for you to remember about why people buy different products or services.

1. People buy benefits and not features.
2. People buy believable claims not simply honest claims.
3. People buy guarantees reputation and good names.
4. People buy solutions to their problems.
5. People buy brand names over unrecognized names.

As you're marketing your products always keep in mind that your customer is always looking for a solution to a problem.

Therefore, you'll want to focus your efforts on being a problem solver for your customer. And remember also to focus on the benefits you supply because customers buy benefits.

Another mindset many entrepreneurs fail to get is that the customer is the most important person to your business. Because when you really look at it the customer is not dependent on you it's you who are dependent on them.

So, when a person comes into your business you don't look at it as if they are somehow interrupting your work because he or she is the purpose for your business.

Can you see the difference in the mindset? It says the objective of your business is to be of service to your customer not the other way around.

If you happen to have a brick and mortar location as a business think about visiting other successful businesses that are similar to yours and see if their offering any special offers or conveniences that you're not and add them to your system. Success leaves clues…right!

Now if you're like me you have an online business and you probably have an online store that you put your products in that you create, right? Well maybe not just yet but you're on the right track keep going.

Have you ever heard the word rapport?

Do you really understand what it means?

Well let me tell you,

Wikipedia who's one of my best friends says rapport is a close and harmonious relationship in which the people or groups concerned understands each other's feelings or ideas and communicate well.

In other words, they respect each other's positions and when you respect someone you have a tendency to want to understand their feeling their ideas and consequently communicate well with them.

That ladies and gentlemen is the relationship that you should strive to achieve with each and every customer whom you cross paths with.

Ok, now back to the online marketing that many of you will be performing, with the internet being the major wheel that will perform most of your marketing efforts it's vital that you understand the most effective places to position the products that you create in front of your audience.

In other words:

- Who is your target market?
- What problem are you solving?
- Who is your competition?

Remember you're creating and marketing (information products) and with that you don't need a location for your customers to come to so getting back to my earlier point about outsourcing certain skills you can see why it's important that you understand but more importantly that you select a strong company to hire when it comes to your marketing efforts.

Now again my friend Wikipedia says the definition of branding is Brand a logo, a name, a slogan, and /a design scheme associated with a product or service. The reason I share this definition with you is you'll want to engrave this short description in your mind and take it with you for the rest of your business life.

Does that sound like I'm asking a lot? Well think about Coke, Nike, Microsoft, and the list goes on, they've all been responsible for having to grow and brand their businesses. Now today the moment you hear Microsoft, Nike, and hundreds of others you automatically know you're talking about a first rate product or service.

Remember, branding is one of the most important aspects of your business whether big of small. You've probably heard me say that your branding is your promise to your customer well what do I mean by that I mean your brand tells your customer what they can expect from your product or service.

Another takeaway from this segment is keep in mind that your brand comes from basically three elements first, who people see or perceive you as being, second, who you are, and finally who you want to become. All three of those will come in handy when you decide to set up your branding strategy.

A simple branding strategy I like to share with beginners consists of 5 different elements.

- How
- What
- Where
- When
- Whom

Whom you plan on communicating and delivering your specific message to.

Other items that are part of your branding strategy are:

1. Where you advertise.
2. Your distribution channels.
3. What you communicate visually and verbally.

Remember you are the orchestrator of all these systems that you'll use in an effort to stand out to be recognized and to become number one.

Now some of the same techniques you used to set up your business plan can also be used when defining your brand.

For example: When you set up your business plan you needed to write out your businesses mission statement well you can use that to define your brand.

As you begin to create your products or services think about the benefits they will provide to your customers that too will help define your brand.

Finally, as you're growing your business what is the perception you want your customers to have of you and your company viewing those items will help with defining your brand also.

Something else I want you to think about now that we are in the information age when someone wants to find out something about you what do they do? Do you know?

They go to our best friend Mr. Google and type in your name the results they get often determine whether or not they will hire you for a specific job they have available. If they're not able to find out anything about you from their Google search what would you think are the chances of them selecting you for the position?

Now when branding yourself you have the luxury of selecting who you want to become or what you want to be known for.

For example; do you want to be known as a motivational speaker, an internet marketer, as a social media expert, or as a professional photographer, as you can see the list is infinite, and all up to you?

Keep in mind that your ultimate goal or objective when creating your brand is to stand out from the rest to have your own unique and specific style or technique that puts you, your products, or your services in demand.

I'm going to give you a few other things you will want to make part of your thought process when establishing your brand.

1. Consider the small details.

Things like the way you respond to emails that you receive the way you respond to new clients the way you dress and so on because they contribute to your brand message.

2. Focus on building your website.

Technology has made it extremely easy to create your own website today by doing so you get to insert specific things in strategic places to brand your strengths, talents, and knowledge about your specific area of expertise.

3. Begin to blog on a regular basis.

Today blogging has become one of the best ways to reach your target audience in an effort to let your new world know who you are and what you do.

Remember too, that branding yourself or your company also increases the value of your company as well as providing your company with motivation and direction for your employees and finally makes customer acquisition much easier.

Lastly in this chapter I want to leave you with six things that branding will do for your company or business.

- Improves Recognition
- Creates Trust
- Supports Advertising
- Builds Financial Value
- Inspires Employees
- Generates New Customers

Now at some point as you're setting the wheels in motion for your new logo, new image, new attitude, and theme, remember words like integrity, honesty, value, commitment, and others because those are the ones you'll want to carry with you throughout your life. They will vicariously help you stay grounded as your business begins to grow.

"As women demanded access to power, the power structure used the beauty myth materially to undermine women's advancement."

— Naomi Wolf

Chapter Nine: Your Friends and Family…

"There is no such thing as a "broken family." Family is family, and is not determined by marriage certificates, divorce papers, and adoption documents. Families are made in the heart. The only time family becomes null is when those ties in the heart are cut. If you cut those ties, those people are not your family. If you make those ties, those people are your family. And if you hate those ties, those people will still be your family because whatever you hate will always be with you."
― C. JoyBell C.

Well, I wanted to save this chapter for close to the end of the book because friends and family are something that most of us have in our lives and we can identify with the different types of them.

You know what I mean some are very supportive, some are sort of supportive, and others aren't supportive at all. Then you have those who would like nothing better than for you to fail.

If I asked you to name me the (one person) in your life that you know you can count on who would that be? _____

If I asked you to name for me the one person in your life that you know you (cannot) count on who would that be? _____ A (TIP) these people shouldn't be the same.

Now that may be a Duh… moment but you would be surprised.

When you're starting your new business, you're going to be experiencing several different emotions you're going to be continually learning more about your business about marketing, about branding and several other skills.

There will be times when you'll want and need to be alone for long periods of time. Your support system needs to be as strong as possible or you need to make adjustments as soon as possible.

Many of the people who are in your immediate family because they don't have the passion that you have or they haven't gained the knowledge that you have will have a very difficult time buying into what you're doing. You need to be ok with that and not try and spend too much time educating them on your plan or strategy.

Now I know when we're dealing with family we're dealing from a place of love and most times unconditional love. But trust me when you're growing a business sometimes that unconditional love must become conditional.

You're doing something that you've never done before and dealing with some of the demands, deadline, and requirements will affect your moods, emotions, and decisions. Therefore, love won't always be a priority you've heard the phrase "nothing personal just business."

Your goal is the success of your business and many times your family simply won't understand when you don't have time to go out for dinner, or take a weekend trip, or even come by and watch a movie.

And remember some of the people you've taken advice from your entire life will see what you're doing and want to give their advice. You must be very conscious of the fact that even though they've given you great advice in the past you are the one who's gaining the knowledge about your business not them and if they're giving their advice based on emotions or a hunch you'll need more specific advice than that.

Another (tip) I want to share with you about family is many times their perception (of time) will throw you off. For instance, if you have the type of family who can sit around and watch television for hours on end chances are they want you to do that also.

Well, again when you're growing a business you must be serious about it. You must be committed to it. And you must know that time wasted is time lost and that needs to matter to you.

Now with all that you may be saying to yourself I'm not going to isolate my family and if I have to in order to become successful I just won't be successful. That's (not) what I'm saying calm down…I'm simply saying just be mindful when those situations arise and they will.

The next thing about family is help your family become an inspiration for your family. I've spent the last five years growing my business and I make it a point to inspire and educate my family members every chance I get when they will let me…

But you know what I've found to be more fulfilling than simply focusing on helping family is becoming an inspiration or guide to others. I've found that there are a lot of people who for whatever reason are afraid to take the next step.

They spend all their time studying the things they need to attending all the classes or seminars they can and even loaded with all that ammunition are afraid to pull the (proverbial trigger).

Perhaps you know someone like that…

I know a lot of someone's like that many are my friends, co-workers, and even people who I meet for the first time I see it in them.

They are frustrated because they've followed the path they've put in the time but they're not getting the results they want or expected.

Why do you think that is? I can tell you this if you ask them a series of questions that get down to the bottom line you'll find time and time again the answer to that question is (themselves).

That's right, they themselves are holding them back. The main reason is of course fear followed closely by not acting when an opportunity presents itself.

Those two things will keep you paralyzed keep you in the same place, and cause you to start to make excuses. Excuses that you know are without merit or facts, and before long making excuses becomes part of your DNA.

You can't allow yourself to fall into that trap you must remain confident that the knowledge you've gained along with your style will get you through. And something else I've found to be amazing is normally it does normally that's enough.

Now am I saying you did the best job you could have done (no) I'm saying you got through it and just like anything else that you're good at right now in the beginning you weren't good at it, it took practice over and over again until you became good at it.

Just know that if you don't stop you will get better however, just like anything else before you can get better you must start…ok.

Before I finish out this chapter I wanted to touch on something that will really impact your vision, your business, and your life in a (negative way) if you don't watch out for it.

And that's your (friends) and (associates).

One of the examples I like to share about those two are imagine today that you won the lottery. Let's say 3 Million dollars really think about that you've won three million dollars.

Who in you circle of friends and associates will benefit from your windfall?

Why have you chosen to give one person more than you're given another? Why have you chosen not to give some people anything? And finally, who in your circle of friends and associates will come with you to the next level because oh yes you are going to another level?

The one thing you must be able to identify is the people who are really in your life for their own agenda not because they care about you and your welfare but because positioning themselves around you will get them to where they want to be faster.

Something else you'll have to deal with are those people in your circle who are now jealous or envious of you and your sudden increase in wealth because there will always be one, two, or more of those.

And finally, what do you do when the friend or associate that you really trusted and put all your faith and trust in betrays you? This you won't know immediately this will take some time just be mindful that it happens. What do you do?

Those are some of the decisions you would have to make instantly if you won the lottery but growing your own business takes a lot more time and will give you the opportunity to see some of the (friends) and (associates) in your life for who and what they really are don't be fooled.

A few of the ways to identify those you (don't) want on your team are:

- Are they always negative?
- Do they lie for no reason?
- Have you seen them steal?
- Does your spirit say they are not good people?
- Can you trust them?
- Are they always trying to upstage you?
- Do they have close friends you know that don't like you?

Those are just a few and I'm sure you can add one or two more but remember this is your business you're trying to grow and you don't want people who are not competent or not in line with your direction to be holding the reins right?

"When we honestly ask ourselves which person in our lives mean the most to us, we often find that it is those who, instead of giving advice, solutions, or cures, have chosen rather to share our pain and touch our wounds with a warm and tender hand. The friend who can be silent with us in a moment of despair or confusion, who can stay with us in an hour of grief and bereavement, who can tolerate not knowing, not curing, not healing and face with us the reality of our powerlessness, that is a friend who cares."

— *Henri J.M. Nouwen*

Chapter Ten: It's who you become that matters…

"I believe that God gives you hopes and dreams in a size that's too large, so you have something to grow into."

— *Lynn A. Robinson*

That's right once you've reached the highest level possible in your area of expertise everything that you've accomplished all the awards, the money, the material possessions, all of it pales in comparison to who you've become.

Now for some people they say how can that be? I mean you're working hard to get the money, the material things, and so on, right?

Well that's true in the sense that the money, the awards, and so forth are by products of success but if you're a knucklehead and you get the money the material possessions and so on you will just become a bigger knucklehead.

It's important that you understand that at the end of the day you're able to look yourself in the mirror and realize that had it not been for the grace of God none of what you have could have been accomplished.

Remember I told you in chapter six about the three things you need to work on daily well if you did work on those daily by the time success knocks on your door you may still be a knucklehead but not so much one.

Because with knowledge comes growth and with growth comes wisdom. Now when I say that realize that nothing is 100% and there will always be the exceptions I'm talking about the rule.

One of the things that I know to be a fact is that the best-informed person has the ability to make the best decisions.

Let me give you an example: you have 2 people both females both 30 years old. Both college graduated and both home owners. The first lady has a plumbing problem in her main bathroom and the second lady has the same problem in her small bathroom.

Neither of them knows anything about plumbing but the second lady grew up in a house full of plumbers, her dad was a plumber, her brother was a plumber, and even her x-husband was a plumber.

Which of those ladies do you think will have the easiest job of getting their plumbing problem solved?

Well, looking at that picture I would say lady number two but what if lady number two lived out of state and her dad, brother, and x-husband, can't get to where she is.

But lady number one is very good at doing research and can Google and find the cheapest and most qualified plumbers in 15 minutes.

Whereas lady number two is not really good with computers and just contacts the first plumber that comes up on her search.

You see the more you're informed about a certain situation or circumstance the better the decisions you'll be able to make. And this is important to know because as you're growing your business there will be times when you won't be able to wait to make a decision it will need to be made now.

Now getting back to who you become one of the things I like to share with my new clients is picture who you are today before you start your business and assess yourself and your growth every six months.

"Beliefs are not related to religion but they are basically about who you are."

— *Stephen Richards*

You'll be surprised how quickly time goes when you're doing something constructive and worthwhile. And when you're actually able to process the fact that you're creating your own online business from scratch it can become overwhelming.

Oftentimes giving you a false sense of who you are and who you've become. We all have our little egos we must deal with but when you combine your ego with success it can very easily turn you into a monster.

Someone that people don't trust or like being around. But because you are successful they either have to be around you because you can open doors for them or they don't know anyone else to help them get to where they're trying to go.

Either way that's not really a good place to be for either of you.

So just be mindful that as you learn as you act on what you've learned and as you begin to receive the benefits of your labor understand that were all people and we all have needs we all have hopes and dreams for ourselves and our families.

And if you can help someone who doesn't have any idea of how to get the results that you have help them…don't be selfish…or stingy…help them…and it will all come back to you at some point.

That's the way it really works here on planet earth. When you give then you get knowing that to be a fact will help keep you grounded which is exactly the way you want to stay, grounded.

Now how do I know this let me share a little bit about my story here before I let you go. Growing up I had zero interest in writing and if there's a number less than zero that's what I had in teaching others what I know.

Today it's my mission and my purpose to gain as much knowledge about my area of expertise and share it with as many people as I possibly can. I love it and I get paid well for doing it.

But more than that I'm providing a service to others who normally may not have someone to model their life or journey through life after. Which is why it's so important for me to live my life in a way that others would want to be like.

Now when I say that does that mean I try to be perfect absolutely not because try as I may it's not possible to attain that position in my mind. However, to be the best I can possibly be is very doable in my mind. And that's what I try and be. The best I can possibly be…or as I like to say "the EXAMPLE" …

Something else, have I always been like this no I haven't it's only been through reading, studying, and acting on what I've learned that I've been able to make the transition to who I am today and I'm truly thankful for the experience…

However, just as blessed as I am others I know as well as you know aren't quite as fortunate.

Which is exactly where you and I come in because sometimes others only need someone who looks like them sounds like them or have had similar experiences as them to make the transition needed to become the best that they can become.

I know it all sounds extremely simple but it's true when you're able to identify what God has given you to contribute to the world whether it be your athletic ability, your intelligence, your compassion, whatever once you can understand just how easy it is to build a business around that your life will immediately change, forever.

The final thing I want to leave you with here today is I want to say thank you for adding more knowledge to what you already know that is the key to your success. However, more important than that focus on specific knowledge (one thing) become an expert at one thing and share everything that you possible can with others about that one thing.

And you can do that through eBooks, Books, Audios, Videos, and other modalities until people in (high places) start to take notice of what you're doing, what happens next is "MAGIC" everything you've ever wanted begins to show up in your life. Everything…just remember, it's who you become that matters…

Now as I like to say on my podcast shows and other places I appear Remember, "Share with someone else, what I've shared with you".

www.ingramcontent.com/pod-product-compliance
Lightning Source LLC
Chambersburg PA
CBHW061148180526
45170CB00002B/677